The Hula Kahiko Collection

Kim Taylor Reece

This book is a collection of my favorite images. Spend some time with them and experience the excitement, allure and beauty of the islands. These images represent my love of paradise and Hawaii.

There is a saying, a picture is worth a thousand words. To describe the images of hula kahiko, Hawaii's ancient dance, could consume even more. To pique your heart and mind, I have chosen just one.

These words are not titles or descriptions—just a springboard, because, as Mark Twain said, *"You can't depend on your eyes, when your imagination is out of focus."*

I hope you enjoy the journey through these pages as much as I have enjoyed creating them.

Aloha,

Kim Taylor Reece

2

anticipate

4

entice

6

immortalize

8

restless

10

exquisite

12

bold

Islands of Hawaii

16

allure

18

passion

20

treasure

22

heroic

24

inspire

26

admire

28

lovely

30

welcome

heavenly

34

motion

36

vulnerable

38

imagine

40

pursue

42

trust

44

mystery

46

grace

48

capture

50

distinct

happiness

54

captivate

56

dream

desire

flirtatious

impetuous

tenderness

66

play

68

journey

70

enchant

72

inviting

fascination

soar

78

beyond

80

believe

82

eternal

84

courage

86

strength

88

celebrate

aloha

Copyright © 2007

Kim Taylor Reece Productions

Sacred Falls, Hawaii, U.S.A.

All rights reserved under copyright convention. No part of this book may be reproduced or transmitted in any form by any means, electronic or mechanical, including copying, recording, or by any information storage or retrieval system, without express written consent from the publisher or copyright holder.

Kim Taylor Reece Gallery

53-866 Kamehameha Highway, Sacred Falls, Hawai'i 96717

www.kimtaylorreece.com

ISBN: 1-59779-033-8

Printed in China